God's little book of
Easter

Words of hope, joy and
new beginnings

Richard Daly

Collins

First published in 2011 by Collins,
an imprint of HarperCollins*Publishers*
77–85 Fulham Palace Road
London W6 8JB

www.harpercollins.co.uk

10 9 8 7 6 5 4 3 2 1

A catalogue record for this book is
available from the British Library

ISBN: 978-0-00-789794-0

Printed and bound in Great Britain by
Martins the Printers Ltd, Berwick upon Tweed

Mixed Sources
Product group from well-managed
forests and other controlled sources
www.fsc.org Cert no. SW-COC-001806
© 1996 Forest Stewardship Council

FSC is a non-profit international organization established to promote the
responsible management of the world's forests. Products carrying the FSC
label are independently certified to assure consumers that they come
from forests that are managed to meet the social, economic and
ecological needs of present and future generations.

Find out more about HarperCollins and the environment at
www.harpercollins.co.uk/green

INTRODUCTION

Easter marks the time for new beginnings.
It's celebrated during the spring, and rings in
the sound of freshness and renewed life. That's
exactly what happened on that resurrection
morning – Christ came forth from the tomb
alive having conquered sin and death, giving
us the perfect gift of eternal life.

This little volume is designed to bring you
hope and renewed strength as you journey
through the various pathways of life with all
its challenges, griefs and fears. This book,
opened at any page, will bring comfort and
assurance whilst reminding you that you
are not alone.

Jesus Christ, who suffered, died and is now alive, wants you to claim his many promises of strength for your life.

May you be inspired by the hope that comes with the meaning of Easter.

ABIDE IN HIM

'He is not here, he is risen!' is probably the greatest
announcement ever made in the history of the
world. Let these words assure you that your God is
not only alive and well, but lives within your heart.

Luke 24:5, 6

MAKE A CHANGE

Easter brings with it a message of hope, promise and a new start for your life. Let this occasion be an opportunity for a new you to come alive.

2 Corinthians 5:17

YOU ARE PRICELESS!

At the cross we discover our true value; for it is there that we discover the price God was willing to pay for us.

1 Corinthians 6:20

THE GREATEST GIFT

The greatest gift is giving at the greatest cost to the least deserving. That's what God did when he gave us Jesus Christ.

James 1:17

LOOK BEYOND THE CROSS

When you have a purpose in life, you will be less
affected by the obstacles that come your way.
Instead of hindrances, they become stepping
stones to success.

Philippians 3:13, 14

YOU'RE WORTH DYING FOR

Everything God made was very good: that means
you too. Endeavour to see yourself as God sees you;
he wants to change your self-image so you can
appreciate your unique gifts and qualities.

Genesis 1:31

HE OVERCAME – YOU CAN TOO

Remember, God is not bound by circumstances, and neither is he overcome by our problems. In every situation he has the power to provide a way out for you. Put your trust in him.

Psalm 121:1–3

ARISE TO A NEW HOPE

Ultimate peace begins when we have peace with
God. Regardless of your past, your future is still
untapped. He is willing to forgive and forget
– just ask him.

1 John 1:9

BE RESTORED

Broken relationships can often lead to broken
hearts. God promises to heal the broken-hearted.
Not only does he heal, he also restores.

Psalm 147:3

TAKE JESUS AT HIS WORD

Jesus said that in three days he would rise again. His
promises never fail – every one of them is like a
precious jewel just waiting to be discovered.

2 Peter 3:9

SEEK YOUR DESTINY

God did not create or redeem you to live a
purposeless existence. He has a customised plan just
for you. Seek it, find it, live it to the full.

Romans 12:6

GIVE AND YOU WILL RECEIVE

Think of all that Christ has done for you – then
share one of these special moments with someone
who needs encouragement. Whatever comfort they
receive will rebound on you.

Luke 6:38

CALL HIM UP

Through prayer you can live in continuous contact
with God. Be encouraged – you will always have
someone on your side.

1 John 2:1

KNOW WHERE YOU'RE GOING

The worst kind of life is one without purpose – with
Christ you get a purpose and a plan to go with it.

Jeremiah 29:11

GROW INTO YOUR DREAMS

Remember dreams always come a size too big, so
you can grow into them. Don't settle for mediocrity.

Mark 9:23

HOLD HIS HAND

Today you are not alone – God is with you. He says,
'I will never leave you, nor forsake you.'

Hebrews 13:5

BELIEVE IN A BIG GOD

God wants you to stretch your faith a little further.
If you want to experience a miracle you have to
step out in faith!

Matthew 9:29

KEEP FOCUSED

You don't have to let fear limit your vision when
God is your source, because his supply is unlimited.

Philippians 4:19

EXPECT A MIRACLE

Just one idea from God, just one, can change your
life and the lives of others. He's got great things in
store for you today – expect them!

Isaiah 55:9

KEEP YOUR HEAD UP

Life can become humdrum and wear you down.
Instead of going around complaining, put a smile on
your face – your altitude changes your attitude.

Philippians 4:1

KNOW YOUR FRIENDS

Solomon said 'A friend loveth at all times,' not just
when you comply with their wishes. Jesus is a friend
who sticks closer than a brother.

Proverbs 17:17

YOU ARE PRECIOUS

Jesus was asked if he could come down from the cross and save himself. Aren't you glad that he sought to save you instead?

Luke 19:10

THE GREATEST SUBSTITUTE

Jesus took our punishment so the Father could embrace us. Now we have a brand new relationship with our Father through grace. Isn't that amazing?

Matthew 8:17

BE COURAGEOUS

Taking a new step is what we fear most, yet our real fear should be standing still. Step forward into growth and development.

Joshua 1:7–9

WASTE NO TIME

Time is an equal opportunities employer. We all get
24 hours, 1440 minutes, 86,400 seconds daily and
we must account for how we use them.

Psalm 90:12

ONE DAY AT A TIME

Worry doesn't rid tomorrow of its challenges,
it robs today of its joy. Remember, God gives
you today's strength for today's needs.

1 Peter 5:7

CLAIM YOUR BREAKTHROUGH

Breaking the habit of a lifetime isn't easy. It requires
an act of real faith and asking God for the courage
to follow through.

Revelation 21:7

GOD KNOWS WHAT HE'S DOING

God doesn't waste anything. He'll use all of your experiences – the good, the bad and the ugly – to prepare you for your next challenge.

Romans 8:28

POWER IN THE BLOOD

Easter says you can put truth in a grave,
but it won't stay there.

(C. W. Hall)

John 8:32

YOU'RE NEVER FORGOTTEN

Jesus will never forget you. You are graven on the
palms of his hands.

Isaiah 49:16

NEW EVERY YEAR

Easter is a promise God gives to each of us each spring. The promise of a new life starts in him.

Lamentations 3:23

FROM DEATH TO LIFE

Christ bore our sins in his body on the cross, but he
died as a victorious saviour. He died as our saviour
but now lives as our Lord.

Revelation 1:8

CHRIST MAKES YOU
A NEW PERSON

The resurrection of Jesus Christ from the dead
changes everything – your past, your present
and your future.

2 Corinthians 5:17

GOD GIVES YOU MORE
THAN YOU ASK

We have been forgiven, redeemed and reconciled to
God our heavenly Father. It's a three-in-one
salvation package.

Matthew 7:7, 8

STAY COOL

Your attitude is like a thermostat – it determines the
climate. If you want to control your climate,
control your attitude.

Philippians 3:21

YOUR HELP IS ASSURED

Jesus came not to be served but to serve. His mission was that of a suffering, humble servant. He turned the whole concept of a lord upside down.

Matthew 20:28

CHOOSE LIFE

God wants us to be happy and joyful. One way this
can be achieved is when we walk straight along the
path the Lord has set before us.

Deuteronomy 30:19

HE IS WITH YOU

Whatever you are facing today, Jesus knows how
you feel. He is fully acquainted with all
our sorrows.

Isaiah 53:3, 4

DRAW NEAR TO GOD

Victory comes when you draw closer to the one who defeated the tempter both in life and in death. So call on him today.

Jeremiah 33:3

RELEASE YOUR POTENTIAL

Jesus knows the worst about you, yet he believes the best in you. He sees you not as you are, but as you will be when he gets through to you.

1 Samuel 16:7

KEEP CLIMBING

Sometimes it might seem that the mountain is too high and we're tempted to give up. That's when we need to listen to his voice: 'Have not I commanded you? Be strong and courageous.'

James 1:12

THE BATTLE IS NOT YOURS

You will never win if you fight in your own strength; so don't even go there. God's already given you authority over all the power that the enemy possesses and nothing shall harm you.

Luke 10:19

1 Samuel 17:4, 7

CHOSEN FROM THE BEGINNING

What God told Jeremiah is true of you: 'Before I
made you in your mother's womb, I chose you,
before you were born I set you apart.'

Jeremiah 1:5

JESUS NEVER FAILS

Having conquered death and the cross, Christ's next mission is to return, this time not as a suffering lamb but as King of kings and Lord of lords.

Psalm 136:3

DON'T LET GO

If you feel scared, you will find total security
when you hold on to the hand of Jesus. He will
never let go of his grip.

Psalm 48:10

Psalm 73:23

YOU'RE BOUGHT WITH A PRICE

Your future is not in the hands of people, it is in the
hands of God. And what he owns he takes care of.

Isaiah 4:1

DON'T SETTLE FOR SECOND BEST

The truth is your accomplishments may bring you some joy, but only in God's presence will you find fullness of joy.

Psalm 16:11

CLAIM YOUR ETERNAL HOME

To the repentant thief on the cross Christ's words
were: 'Today you shall be with me in paradise.'
It's a promise that speaks to you – claim your
paradise today.

John 14:1–3

YOU'RE LOVED BEYOND MEASURE

To the chanting mob the dying Christ said: 'Father,
forgive them, for they know not what they do.'
Even in his suffering, he still reached out to cover
the sins of his accusers. What selfless love!

Jeremiah 31:3

DON'T DESPAIR

Our God, who is 'the beginning and the end',
sees things in their completed state, including
your ultimate victory.

Revelation 22:13

YOUR FORMULA FOR SUCCESS

For every battle God has a strategy. Don't just
pray about the battle – ask God to show you
the plan for victory.

Judges 6:16

IF GOD IS FOR YOU …

Your God is greater than any opposition
you are facing!

Romans 8:31

GIVE PRAISE TO GOD

God loves to start with nothing, for then there's
no doubt about who has the power and who
gets the credit!

John 15:5

BE A CONQUEROR

Life is about overcoming! When you've conquered
one mountain, before you know it you're faced with
the next – a bigger one. Remember the battle's
not yours, but God's.

1 John 4:4

LET BYGONES BE BYGONES

Who do you need to forgive today? Forgive them!
Or at least ask God to help you start the process.
The person who truly walks with God is a person
who is merciful and forgiving.

Matthew 6:14

Psalm 86:5

TAKE ANOTHER LOOK

Don't look at the way things are and ask 'Why?'
Look at the way things could be and ask 'Why not?'

Matthew 19:26

BE AVAILABLE

Through the power of God's indwelling spirit you
can make a difference. Just make yourself available
to God and let him show you what he can do
with your life.

Philippians 3:13, 14

JUST BELIEVE

Assurance of a place in heaven comes only through accepting Jesus as your personal saviour, believing that he died for your sins and rose again to give you everlasting life. No more is needed, no less will get you in.

John 3:16

DEVELOP AN ATTITUDE
OF GRATITUDE

Begin thanking God today for what he's done and
what he's going to do on your behalf, because he
will come through for you.

Psalm 92:1

Ephesians 5:20

LET GOD RULE

Stop trying so hard to make things happen on your terms, and begin allowing God to make things happen for you on his terms.

Proverbs 3:5, 6

DON'T BE SIDETRACKED

When you're doing anything worthwhile, expect
opposition from those who aren't privy to God's
plan in your life. That goes with the job.

Proverbs 16:7

SEEK GODLY WISDOM

The decisions you make today will affect not
only you but future generations – so seek God
to make the right move.

Proverbs 4:5

HANG ON IN THERE

Just because it hasn't happened yet, this doesn't mean God has changed his mind. While you are waiting, God is still working.

James 1:4

ACCEPT GOD'S TIMING

If you're asking God to make you bigger instead of better, you may be disappointed. God won't give you what you're not ready to handle.

Luke 16:10

LET HIM MOULD YOU

Remember you are still a work in progress – God's
not finished with you yet!

Jeremiah 18:4

PROVE YOUR LOVE

Loving God is a commitment, an attitude resulting in action, a focus, a daily decision to acknowledge him in your life. So … do you love God?

Revelation 2:4

CAST YOUR BURDENS ON HIM

Our capacity for handling stress is limited and
preventing stress is always better than trying to deal
with it. So cast all your cares on the Lord –
he will sustain you!

Matthew 11:28, 29

ACCEPT GOD'S PARDON

Jesus came to let you know that the penalty of sin has been removed and its power is broken. In God's eyes, you're loved and accepted!

Nehemiah 9:17

DON'T BE HARD ON YOURSELF

If God is willing to pardon your mistakes and even
bury them, isn't time you stopped beating yourself
up? Receive his grace and move on!

Philippians 3:13

DON'T STAY DOWN

Falling down is just a part of learning to walk.
Don't be discouraged – God is still at work in your
life, so get up and try again.

Proverbs 24:16

THINK POSITIVELY

Think excellent thoughts! Whatever enters your
mind repeatedly occupies, shapes and controls it,
and in the end expresses itself in who you are
and what you do.

Philippians 4:8

BUILD ON SOLID GROUND

God's love for us is set in concrete. That's the
foundation you build your life on.

Romans 8:39

DON'T BE OVERWHELMED

God has a purpose behind every problem. But he also has a protective shield in front of it.

Romans 8:28

Ecclesiastes 3:17

TRUST GOD'S WAY

God often uses circumstances to accomplish his will.
The reason is obvious; we face circumstances
24 hours a day.

1 Peter 1:7

TURN OBSTACLES INTO STEPPING STONES

Adversity draws us closer to God. There are things
we learn about God when we're in trouble that we
can't learn any other way. But remember, 'The Lord
is close to the broken-hearted.'

Psalm 34:18

LET GO

Submitting the situation to God and trusting him with the means and timing is hard for most of us to do. Why? Because it means giving up control, but remember he won't fail you!

James 4:7

THINK BIG

Big oak trees grow from little acorns. When you
discover your God-given dream and commit to it,
there's no telling how far you'll go or what
impact you'll make.

Matthew 21:21

LET GOD LEAD

Stop trying to control every possible outcome! Life is much more peaceful when you decide to stand on God's word and trust him, regardless of circumstances.

Proverbs 3:7

BE PATIENT IN WAITING

Patience is what God gives you when bad things
remain unchanged. It's faith taking its time.

Romans 5:3

STAY CALM

Next time you get all worked up, ask yourself,
'What is the enemy trying to do here?' Do your
utmost to exercise self-control and remain in peace.

Ephesians 4:27

LIVE TO THE MAX

Christ's desire for you is that in this world you
live your life to the full.

John 10:10

KEEP YOUR EYES ON JESUS

God's message of salvation is very clear.
'Look to me and be saved … For I am God
and there is no other.'

Isaiah 45:22

BE REUNITED

Atonement is the term for us being reconciled to
God through Christ's sacrifice. It allows us to
experience 'at-one-ment' with our Lord once again.

Romans 5:11

GOD CAN HANDLE IT

The scriptures present Christ as the sin-bearer of
the human race. Now that's a load of sins placed
on his shoulders.

Isaiah 53:6–12

2 Corinthians 5:20, 21

WASHED IN THE BLOOD

When we come to God in repentance he does not
see us dressed in our sinful garments. He sees
Christ's robe of righteousness covering us and
we are pronounced redeemed, cleansed and
clean in his Spirit.

Isaiah 61:10

YOU CAN DO IT!

Christ's life provides the assurance that we can live victoriously. You can do all things through Christ who strengthens you.

Philippians 4:13

THE JOY OF EASTER

Good Friday will remain 'good' because of what happened on Easter Sunday.

1 Corinthians 15:17

DEPEND ON HIM

God will never give you an assignment you can
complete without his help, so don't even try it alone.

2 Samuel 22:3

YOU ARE NOT ALONE

Many are the afflictions of the righteous but the
Lord delivers him out of them all. 'When you can't
see him, his eyes are always on you!'

Psalm 34:19

YOU'VE BEEN RESTORED

While we were distant from God, he came
down to be our friend.

Proverbs 18:24

UNDESERVED FAVOUR

In Christ we are not only pardoned but acquitted
and declared righteous.

Romans 5:6–10

EASTER SUNDAY'S BLESSING

It is nothing that we have done but everything
Christ has done that makes us worthy.

Titus 3:5

STAY AT THE FEET OF JESUS

No matter how sinful your past life is, how far you've strayed or how low you've stooped – there's still room at the cross of Jesus for you.

Ephesians 1:7

LET GOD REMAKE YOU

Only the creator who created something out of nothing can transform your life. He can take your nothing and make you something.

1 Thessalonians 5:23

CONTROL YOUR THOUGHTS

Whoever occupies our mind, occupies us.
That's why God says, 'let this mind be in you
that was in Christ Jesus.'

2 Corinthians 10:5

RESURRECTION HOPE

When Christ said those final words, 'It is finished,' it ushered in the start of a new life for us.

1 Peter 1:23

DON'T RUN AHEAD OF GOD

God will not accelerate his pace to catch up with
ours. We need to slow down in order to get back
into step with him.

Psalm 46:10

DON'T GIVE UP!

Endurance means staying the course. Jesus 'endured the cross' – he completed the course so that we can be winners.

James 1:3

LET GOD RECREATE YOU

God loves to take the lost, the last, the least and the lowest and make them into something beautiful. To him you are the apple of his eye.

Zechariah 2:8

2 Corinthians 5:17

EXPECT GREAT THINGS TO COME

Don't you know that God has more for you?
If you trust him with your future, your best
days are yet to come!

Isaiah 43:18, 19

FORGIVE AS YOU HAVE
BEEN FORGIVEN

Practising forgiveness stems from a deep gratitude
to God for wiping out a debt so great, we could
never have repaid it.

Luke 23:24

TRUST GOD COMPLETELY

When Jesus said to his Father, 'into your hands I commit my spirit,' that was a cry of surrender and trust to the Father.

Luke 23:46

YOU'VE BEEN SET FREE

With Jesus being a ransom for us, God wrote, 'paid in full' over every sin you've committed, from the womb to the tomb.

Colossians 2:13, 14

THE FUTURE IS BRIGHT

Jesus does not penalise us for our past, locking us into it forever. Knowing the worst about us, he still believes the best.

Jeremiah 31:17

Jeremiah 29:11

BASK IN THE LOVE OF GOD

Nothing can change the way God feels about you.
Nothing can alter the fact that he will continue to
love you regardless of what you do or say.

Songs 8:7

LET GOD START AFRESH

From the resurrection we can see that God causes
dead things to come alive. What needs to come
alive in your life today?

Colossians 3:1

STAY BLESSED

What's so amazing about grace? The fact that you
are alive right now and he's keeping you
breathing each day is amazing!

Acts 15:11

1 Corinthians 15:11

YOU ARE SPECIAL

Jesus could have called 10,000 angels but he
died alone for you and me.

1 Peter 3:8

YOU'RE SAVED BY GRACE

What makes you a Christian is not perfection,
it's God's forgiveness.

Romans 5:15

LET NOT YOUR HEART BE TROUBLED

Easter can bring hope to a person devastated with the loss of a loved one. It brings the promise of a heavenly reunion.

John 14:1–3

REST IN HIS ARMS

The word 'Abba' simply means 'Daddy'. How
wonderful! He simply wants us to come to him at
any time, crawl into his lap, feel secure in his
everlasting arms and call him 'Daddy'.

Romans 8:15

YOU MEAN EVERYTHING TO HIM

If God didn't hesitate to put everything on the line
for you, is there anything else he wouldn't
gladly do for you?

Romans 8:39

PREDESTINED TO BE SAVED

God didn't choose you because you're a wonderful
person. He chose you because he wanted to.

Ephesians 1:5

LIGHT OF THE WORLD

When Jesus was crucified the earth was plunged
into darkness. But on Easter morning the light
came on – for ever.

2 Samuel 22:29

IT'S NOT TOO LATE

You can't do anything about your past, but starting
today you can do something about your future –
one choice and one act at a time.

Job 14:14–17

CLAIM HIS PROMISES

Jesus is the only man ever to make an appointment beyond the grave and show up for it. You can be assured he always keeps his promises.

John 11:25

TURN YOUR MOURNING
INTO DANCING

Christ's resurrection guarantees ours. If you have
experienced the heartache of burying those you
love, Easter guarantees you'll meet them again,
alive, immortal, glorified and just like Jesus!

1 Thessalonians 4:16, 17

BE CONTENT

Happiness is not about getting what you want, it's about enjoying what you've got! So keep your perspective and be grateful every day.

1 Timothy 6:8

LIVE LIFE INTENTIONALLY

God has a plan and a destiny for your life.
Living according to his will unlocks these
pathways to eternity.

Proverbs 16:9

Proverbs 19:21

RISE AND SHINE

Today the greatest announcement still speaks from
the tomb: 'He is not here, he is risen!'

Luke 24:6

HE'S INCREDIBLE

Sin could not overpower him, suffering could not prevent him, death could not hold him and the tomb could not contain him. Don't you want him by your side?

Jeremiah 32:27

BE WASHED

Would you be free from your burden of sin?
There's power in the blood, power in the blood!

L. E. Jones

Revelation 1:5

LET HIM IN

Today Jesus says, 'Behold I stand at the door and knock. If anyone hears my voice I will come in and eat with him and he with me.'

Romans 3:20, 21

PUT CHRIST FIRST

Your priorities determine how you spend your time,
so set them prayerfully and maintain them carefully.

Psalm 90:12

SEEK GODLY WISDOM

Each choice is a crossroads in life, one that will
either confirm or compromise your commitment.
Let your integrity be the gauge of the direction
you choose.

John 10:27

HOLD ON

Nothing in my hand I bring,
simply to your cross I cling.

A. M. Toplady

1 Timothy 6:12

BE HEAVENWARD BOUND

The biggest fact about Joseph's tomb was that it was not a tomb at all; it was a room for a transient. Jesus just stopped there ... on his way back to glory.

H. B. Smith

1 Corinthians 15:55

JESUS PAID IT ALL

He wept and mourned so we can laugh and rejoice.
He was apprehended that we might escape. He was
betrayed that we might go free.

John Bunyan

1 Corinthians 6:20

SEALED FOR LIFE

Jesus cannot forget us; we are sealed with the
promise of the Holy Spirit.

Ephesians 1:13

THE ULTIMATE SACRIFICE

No pain, no palm;
no thorns, no throne;
no gall, no glory;
no cross, no crown.

William Penn

Hebrews 12:2

COUNT YOUR BLESSINGS

1 cross
2 thieves
3 nails
4 given

Genesis 49:25, 26

GOD KNOWS ALL

Only God could have remembered
through the winter, cold and grey
how to renew the earth with beauty
and give us Easter day.

Helen Steiner Rice

Job 21:22

CELEBRATE YOUR EASTER

On Easter morn he showed he is our saviour.
His resurrection proves he is our Lord.
That is why we tell you 'Happy Easter';
he secured our heavenly reward.

Joanna Fuchs

1 Corinthians 1:18

THE GREATEST STORY

The best of the story is the very last part;
It's why on Easter we're filled with pleasure.
Death could not our saviour hold;
his power is beyond all measure.

Joanna Fuchs

Matthew 1:21

BE FREE IN CHRIST

Without showing mercy, life becomes an endless
cycle of resentment and retaliation. But as you walk
in love, you experience freedom.

Colossians 3:13

DON'T STAY DOWN

Regardless of how often you've been knocked down, God always offers you his almighty hand to pick you up, clean you up and give you a chance to begin again.

Psalm 51:2

BE STILL AND KNOW

Following Jesus can't be done at a sprint; you can't
go faster than the one who's leading, so slow down,
don't rush ahead – spend time with him!

Matthew 11:28

YOU'RE WORTH IT

Just think; the God of the universe willingly left the
splendour of heaven, was born into poverty and
died on a cruel cross for wayward humanity. Why?
Because that's how much you mean to him!

Romans 6:7

YOU ARE UNIQUE!

If you were the only one in need of salvation in the entire world, Jesus would have gone through all that he did just for you! What amazing love!

Romans 5:15

LET HIM FIND YOU

Contrary to popular opinion, God does not wait for you to come to him. God comes to seek and find you. He will never let you go.

Psalm 139:7

GOD'S MIND IS MADE UP!

There is nothing we can do to make God love
us more. There is nothing we can do to make
God love us less.

Philip Yancey

John 3:16

THE SUFFERING SERVANT

He was wounded for our transgressions, bruised for
our iniquities; the chastisement for our peace was
upon him, and by his stripes we are healed.

Isaiah 53:5

PROTECTED FROM THE ENEMY

When God looks at you, he sees only the one who
surrounds you! Because you're in Christ your
victory is secure. You can rejoice!

Zechariah 3:3, 4

OPEN YOUR HEART

It's impossible to be merciful until we've thoroughly come to terms with our own need for mercy and received it from the Lord.

Lamentations 3:22, 23

DEDICATE YOURSELF TO JESUS

What you are is God's gift to you; what you do with
yourself is your gift back to him.

2 Corinthians 9:15

SEEK YE FIRST

Today, ask God to show you his priorities for your life, and then set your personal goals accordingly. There's no feeling like knowing you're doing the right thing at the right time.

Matthew 6:33

REMEMBER HOW HE LED YOU

With God a delay is not a denial. Remember how
far you've come, not just how far you have to go.
You may not be where you want to be, but neither
are you where you used to be.

John 1:4

GO THE EXTRA MILE

Want to experience a miracle? Then be willing to
stretch your faith a little more. Put God to the test!

Malachi 3:10

MAKE A CHANGE WITHIN

If there's any cross we are to carry, it is the cross of self-denial and submitting our will to the all-wise God.

Matthew 16:24

YOU CAN START AGAIN

Baptism means 'to immerse' – what a wonderful representation of Christ's death, burial and resurrection! We come up out of the water and we are a new creation. The old things have passed away, the new has come.

Romans 6:4

BE COMFORTED

One of the titles of the Holy Spirit is 'comforter'. It means 'to be called to the side of' – when we lose a loved one we have the assurance from the God of all comfort that he will be with us.

2 Corinthians 1:3, 4

PUT GOD TO THE TEST

Ask great things and expect great things from God.
He is faithful and will fulfil his promises.

Luke 6:38

DO WHAT GOD ASKS

'What does the Lord require of you but to do
justice, to love mercy and to walk humbly
with your God?'

Micah 6:8

LET NATURE TESTIFY OF GOD

Our Lord has written the promise of the
resurrection, not in books alone, but in
every leaf in springtime.

Martin Luther

Psalm 91:1

JOY COMES IN THE MORNING

The darkest hour is just before the dawn.
Be encouraged – the sun will shine again.
God won't fail you!

Psalm 30:5

GOING UP YONDER

Why should we grieve when our loved ones die?
for we'll meet them again in a cloudless sky;
for Easter is more that a beautiful story,
it's the promise of a life of eternal glory.

Revelation 21:4